Machines are the easy part; people are the hard part:

Observations about making technology work in schools

Written by Doug Johnson

Illustrated by Brady Johnson

Blue Skunk Press
A Beaver's Pond Press Book
Cleveland MN
© 2004

ISBN 1-59298-070-8

Library of Congress Catalog Number: 2004107763

Printed in the United States of America

First Printing: June 2004

07 06 05 04 03 6 5 4 3 2 1

Beaver's Pond Press, Inc.

7104 Ohms Lane, Suite 216
Edina, MN 55439-2129
(952) 829-8818
www.BeaversPondPress.com

to order, visit www.BookHouseFulfillment.com or call 1-800-901-3480. Reseller discounts available.

Advanced reviews from people who ought to know better:

"Every field should have a little book of wisdom to guide it. Doug Johnson's *Machines are the Easy Part* delivers practical truths and a welcome dose of humor for ed tech leaders (we geeks long in need of affirmation and smiles). You'll share these stories with your colleagues; you'll refer to them when the funding fails and the network crashes. You'll smile, you'll nod, you'll want to go out there and be a better leader. Bravo, Doug!"—Joyce Valenza, techlife@school columnist, *Philadelphia Inquirer* and author of *Power Research Tools.*

"Doug Johnson's newest book proves the old adage that dynamite comes in small packages. *Machines Are the Easy Part* packs powerful truths into simple examples, stimulating quotations, and humorous quips. Have a highlighter in hand because you'll want to remember line after line. I laughed and shouted 'Amen' as I simultaneously read it and thought about who needed to read it next!"—Debbie Silver dsilver@bayou.com author of *Drumming to the Beat of a Different Marcher: Finding the Rhythm for Teaching a Differentiated Classroom.*

"Common sense, wit and sound advice are in short supply these days, but Doug Johnson's little book is overflowing with all three. A tasty treat worth dropping on certain folks' desk tops."—Jamie McKenzie, author of the e-journal "From Now On" www.fno.org and book *Planning Good Change*.

Table of Contents

Forward: the true miracle of the Pyramids | xii

General rules

Change rules and job security

Technology rules

Writing and presenting rules

Administration of anything rules

Teaching rules

Library rules

59. The number of students in the media center will always be in inverse proportion to the importance of anyone stopping by for a visit. | **83**

60. Life-long impressions of libraries are formed very young. | **84**

61. The Library Rule rule. | **85**

62. The librarian is the library. | **86**

63. The paraprofessional is often the face of the library. | **87**

64. There is no reason not to have a budget. | **88**

65. Be virtual. | **89**

66. Accentuate the things you can do that the Internet can't. | **90**

67. Be a teacher first, a librarian second. | **91**

68. Don't advocate for libraries. | **92**

69. Poor librarians reflect on all of us. | **93**

70. Weed | **94**

Parting thoughts

Forward: the true miracle of the Pyramids

I once visited the Great Pyramids of Giza and have always remembered an observation made by the Qaddafi look-alike tour guide:

> "Most people marvel at the engineering and building when looking at these ancient wonders. But the true miracle was the sophistication of human management 4,000 years ago. How did this early civilization feed, house, train, organize and motivate the workers in order to complete these giant undertakings?"

Many books and articles on educational technology focus on the equipment itself—what software to use, how to create and manage networks; how to write lesson plans that incorporate technology; what technology skills students need—all of it sprinkled with a generous dose of TLAs (Three Letter Acronyms). Heavy on the machines; light on the humanity.

This little book takes a somewhat different approach to educational technology. Its focus is on the human elements to which attention must be paid before technology can have an impact on teaching and learning.

The book is designed to be read in one sitting or in lots of little sittings. (I know where I will be keeping my copy!) It doesn't replace anything already available. It's not definitive on any topic.

But it is my hope that it will appeal to those of you who prefer to think about technology only a healthy amount of your waking lives, and reassure those of you who are top-notch educators without being technology gurus; that it will make you think, give you an insight, and perhaps a chuckle or two as well. No "feature creep" here.

General rules

An expert is someone who has a somewhat defensible position but can state it with extraordinary confidence.

Why should you believe anything you are about to read? Maybe you shouldn't.

To my credit, I have had a pretty good education, have had moderate success in the field of education, and have managed to convince quite a few people to publish things I've written. But that is about it.

Be warned: My school doesn't make many headlines. My income still requires that I pay my overdrafts one dollar at a time. My personal life should be nobody's model (although I've enjoyed it.)

Agree or disagree with any of my observations. Feel free to say "I've said that myself a million times." Get mad enough to write your own book.

But have fun reading this.

It's always, always, always better to be a nice person than an ass.

You will make mistakes at home and on the job, so keep this in mind: People will forgive your mistakes if you are generally a nice person; they never forget them if you behave like an ass.

One of my technicians once warned a teacher: "I am beginning to think it is easier to make you mad than to make you happy. Remember, you are a lot more fun to watch when you are mad." The teacher got nicer.

Go with the person, not the firm.

We once hired a company to do a network installation and it did a bang-up job. We hired the same company a year later and it did the worst work we had ever encountered. During the course of the year, one guy, the guy who did the first job for us, had quit. Don't trust companies—trust the people in them.

A corollary says that the worst schools have good teachers in them and the best schools have poor teachers in them. It seems a folly to worry a lot about what school your children go to. Just make sure they get the best teachers in the school.

4

Even when hiding feels good, don't do it.

The best way to be seen as valuable, especially in an administrative or supervisory position, is to go out and talk to the people your department serves, find out what's bugging them about your area of responsibility, and then find ways to reduce the irritation.

As I walk through the buildings in my district, I like to think of myself as a giant "complaint magnet." I write down every problem I hear about and then either solve it or find out why it can't be solved. I always communicate back to the person who had the problem outlining what I've done.

Even if I haven't been of much help, people like to know they have been heard.

5

The race is not always to the swift, but to those who keep on learning.

The moral of Aesop's tale about the tortoise and the hare is that the race is not always to the swift, but to those who keep on running. I agree.

But you can't just keep running without ever changing course. To run in the right direction you always have to be on a fairly high learning curve. Read, listen, read, go to conferences, read, research, read, and read some more.

Now, I am a very lazy professional reader. I'd much rather escape into a good mystery or a work of historical fiction. The deal I made with myself is to alternate between professional books and recreational books. Now, if only the serious books would read as fast as a Harry Bosch mystery!

6

Never assume.

Never assume the computer will work with the projector. Never assume your wife is picking up the milk. Never assume your job is secure. Never assume that other people will vote for the politician you want in office and never assume the politicians will vote for your cause. Never assume someone else will play a leadership role in your profession. Never assume the world will be just fine without you doing something about the problems in it.

It takes just seconds to double check things. I think I learned this one cold winter afternoon when I sat expecting my wife to meet me at the Hardee's in New Hampton, Iowa, while she was sitting all afternoon at the Hardee's in Hampton, Iowa.

Never assume that it is OK to assume even once.

Change rules and job security

Change is inevitable—except in human nature.

People have been grouching about change for a very long time. Just accept it and change what needs changing.

The Renaissance philosopher Machiavelli said ". . . it ought to be remembered that there is nothing more difficult to take in hand, more perilous to conduct, or more uncertain in its success, than to take the lead in the introduction of a new order of things, because the innovator has for enemies all those who have done well under the old conditions, and lukewarm defenders in those who may do well under the new."

The very best way I've found to get people to stop complaining about a particular thing is to give them something new to complain about. That's one good reason to update your computer systems every now and again. Maybe it's the only good reason.

Change anything and someone is not going to like it.

But some people will. The real key to getting people to accept a new way of doing things is to highlight the WIIFM (What's In It For Me) factors. You must convince people that the new policy, technology, or plan is:

- Going to make their jobs easier
- Going to make them more efficient
- Going to make them more effective, or
- Going to . . . no, it has to be one of the previous three.

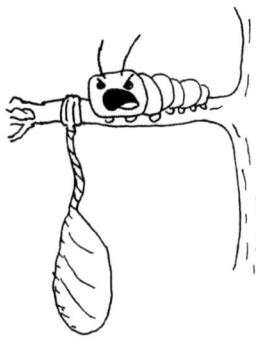

If the change doesn't result in one of these things happening, you might want to question what exactly *your* motive is for asking people to make the change. To make YOUR life easier is not sufficient reason.

The two things you need to make any kind of change are a thick skin and a mission from God.

All of us are sensitive to criticism. I can read a hundred workshop evaluation forms and manage to only remember the three or four that were less than enthusiastic. That's the way most people are made. But you must take your shots along with the praise.

What helps deflect the arrows is faith that what you are doing is in the best interest of others. (Or as the Blues Brothers put it: "We're on a mis-sion from God.") Without this faith in yourself and what you do, it won't take much to turn you back.

I think Ambrose Red-moon said it best: "Cour-age is not the absence of fear, but the judgment that something else is more im-portant than fear."

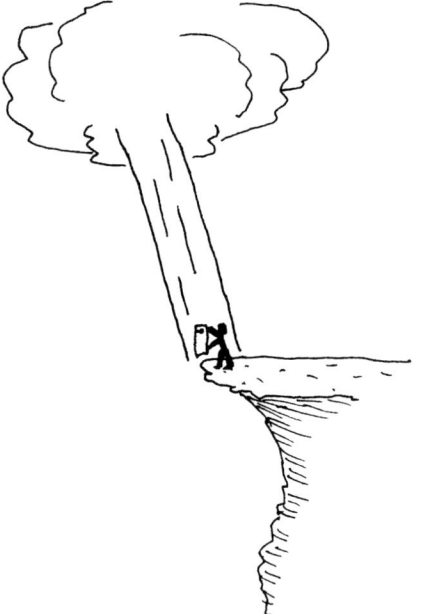

10

Change can only be made by the rank and file.

A tour guide in Nairobi told me this tale about how the Ngong (Knuckle) Hills came into being.

A giant once ravished the land. The animals of the savanna were determined to get rid of it. The big animals went in first: the elephants, the rhinos, the lions, one after the other. Each was soundly trounced.

That night all the ants gathered and decided each would carry a few clumps of dirt and place them on the giant while he was asleep. By the next morning the giant was buried so deeply that he never rose again. All that can be seen today are the protruding knuckles of one hand—the Ngong Hills.

Who can make more improvements in education: The Department of Education or many teachers making small changes?

II

You always have to do something else before you can do what you want to do.

Schools ignore attention to infrastructure at a high cost. Putting high-speed computers in the classroom without thinking about network speed and capacity, security, and teacher training is like buying a Ferrari for someone who lives on a dirt road and can't drive.

Without reliable networks, good tech support and a degree of personal comfort at the keyboard, teachers will not use technology—period. We are foolish to insist that teachers have a "backup plan in case the technology doesn't work."

You think they don't have enough to do without creating *two* sets of lesson plans?

Technology has to be adequate, reliable, and secure if it's to be used.

12

Teaching is harder than ever.

I have worked in education for over twenty-five years and am happy to report that today I work with better teachers, in better facilities, using better resources, and seeing better results than at any other time in my career.

I have also never felt my profession more heavily criticized by politicians and the press. Why?

It simply boils down to the fact that being well-educated—knowing how to communicate, to solve problems using information, and to work productively with others—is no longer optional for anyone in the current workforce. The no-brainer jobs have been taken by robots or by workers in developing countries.

It's not that we are not doing better. It's that we are not doing better fast enough.

Research can tell you anything you'd like to hear.

Shakespeare once wrote: "The devil can cite Scripture for his purpose." Were he alive today, he might have said, "The devil can cite Statistics for his purpose."

The current drive for "data-driven decision making" concerns me because

- Few educators REALLY have the training to make good judgments based on data (quick—define "standard deviation from the norm," "statistically significant," or "T-score")
- Data-gathering efforts can be constructed or interpreted to meet political ends
- We overvalue those things in education that can be measured.

Of course, I *like* the research that backs up my observations, gut feelings and philosophy. And, by golly, I'll keep looking until I find it.

First Rule of Job Security: Find out what problems are keeping your boss from sleeping well at night.

If you can't list the top three things that your supervisor worries about, your job may be vulnerable.

My boss, Ed the superintendent, worries about finances and public perception of the effectiveness of our district; he also worries, (bless his heart) about whether all our kids are getting the best education possible.

Now it is my job to:

- Honestly work toward helping relieve Ed's worries
- Make sure he knows of those efforts

What keeps *your* boss awake at night?

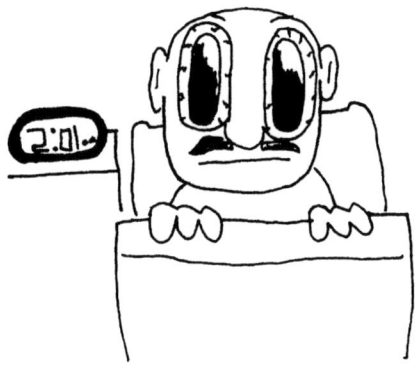

15

Remember the Drill Bit Rule

An old maxim states: "People don't buy a drill bit because they want a drill bit; they buy it because they want a hole."

- You don't buy technology because you want technology; you buy it because you want a more effective school.
- You don't have a library for the sake of having a library; you have a library because you want better-educated kids.

Too often we confuse the thing with the reason for the thing, much to our own peril. Having a computer on every desk is not a goal. Having x number of books in the library is not a goal. These may be means to reach a goal, but they are not the goal itself.

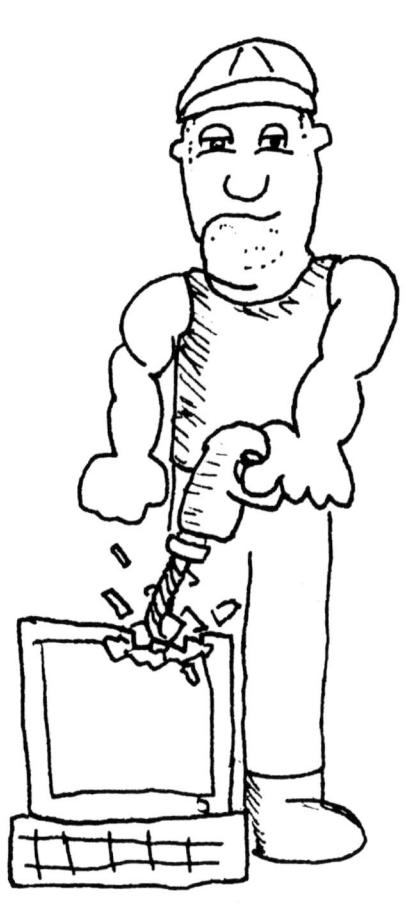

16

We can no longer afford to only work with the living.

The standing advice for achieving success in staff development activities has been:

WORK WITH THE LIVING.

A parent once approached me at an open house. "You're the technology director," she confirmed. "I just love what Miss Smith is doing with the third graders in her classroom. The computer-created booklets, the keypal project, the video-taped presentations—all of it. These are good skills that kids need."

"Thanks," says I, puffing up a bit.

"But here is my problem," the parent continued. "My little Susie has Mr. Brown for her third grade teacher and Mr. Brown wouldn't know a computer if it bit him in the butt. When are *you* going to do something about that?"

Parents feel that their childrens' technology and information-literacy skills are so important that they're uncomfortable leaving to chance the possibility of getting a technology-savvy teacher.

We've got to start having reasonable technology-use expectations of all teachers—not just those with respiration.

17

The importance of teacher quality.

It's my job to see that technology is effectively used by teachers and students in the district. I "advocate" for its use for the simple reason that my job depends on it. And I'm rather fond of my job.

But here is my problem. Now and again I run into an absolutely terrific teacher who utterly despises technology. These modern-day Platos get kids passionate about learning, begin important discussions that carry on into the hallway and sometimes on into the weekends, and somehow instill not just facts or skills, but true knowledge and even wisdom in their students.

Most parents would rather their children had a great teacher with mediocre technology than a mediocre teacher with great technology.

I don't try very hard to "improve" the truly gifted teachers with technology.

18

If you can't afford the whole cure, don't even start it.

I call this the Antibiotic Law of Educational Change.

If you get a prescription to kill a germ, you are sternly warned to keep taking the medicine until it is gone—not just until the symptoms disappear. If you don't, the bug can come back, strengthened by new resistance to the antibiotic.

We in education kill ourselves by ignoring this rule. We formulate a budget for a program, a grant, or a project then happily accept less than the full amount of the funding request *without changing the promised result*. We then get half-assed results that demoralize the participants and increase the skepticism of those who funded us.

Don't accept project funding if it is not for the full amount or make clear that the reduced amount will affect the outcome, and redefine your objectives.

No parent has ever had an ugly baby.

Ask any group of people if they themselves are the parents of an ugly baby. No one is.

Ask the same group of people if they have ever *seen* an ugly baby. Nearly all the hands go up.

This phenomenon is why all of us need reality checks of our programs, our policies, and our teaching styles. The things we do usually look pretty darned good to us.

Who can tell us if we have an "ugly baby" that we may not be aware of?

- Advisory groups
- Outside evaluators
- Anonymous surveys
- National or state standards

It's in our students' best interest to get an objective opinion on the things to which we are closest.

Technology rules

20

Machines are the easy part; people are the hard part.

The very best technologist is a good psychologist. The skills needed to create a system, write software, or operate a piece of technology are all teachable: they may be complex and praiseworthy, but they are completely teachable. The task is akin to training a circus dog to ride a bicycle.

But technology plans often fail in schools even when the school has people who can put the "stuff" in place, because the training doesn't measure up to the equipment, and then all this lovely stuff sits around gathering dust, or is used by a pathetically small group of technology enthusiasts.

The book *Crossing the Chasm* (HarperBusiness, 2002) by Geoffrey A. Moore does as fine a job as I've seen explaining how to have new innovations adopted by nearly everyone in an organization.

Read it.

Beware the law of unintended consequences.

The full impact of adopting a technology can never be fully predicted. (Just read any Michael Crichton novel.)

- Give kids access to the Internet, and they download term papers.
- Ask that all work be word-processed, and paper and toner bills skyrocket.
- Give students a good means of sharing information electronically, and electronic cheating becomes widespread.
- Give parents real-time access to their children's progress, and teachers become overwhelmed with e-mail.

Now, smart person that you are, you're probably thinking, "And you didn't plan for this?" Nope, these things took me by surprise.

View technology as the evil genie from *1001 Arabian Nights*. You can get what you ask for—but it always comes with strings attached.

"Explain it to me like I was 6 years old."

A common Murphy's Law states: "Technology is dominated by those who manage what they do not understand."

As an English major and former librarian who is sometimes less than technically astute and always has to sing in a soft voice "Righty tighty, lefty loosey" when encountering anything with threads, I always worry that Murphy had me in mind when he wrote the law.

To counteract this, I try to remember Denzel Washington's great line in the movie *Philadelphia,* "Explain it to me like I was 6 years old." My frustrated technicians have sometimes worked with me for a very long time, drawing pictures, forming analogies, and searching for ever shorter words to describe functions and reasons for technologies.

Don't make decisions about things you don't understand. Develop an understanding no matter how long it takes.

23

What technology first makes possible, it soon makes imperative.

Did you notice that soon after one bank got online banking, every bank was offering it?

This is also happening with parent access to grades, web-accessible library catalogs, and the ability to pay school bills online. Parents (and the general public) now expect a school's schedules, lunch menus, contact information for staff (including staff e-mail) and other "services" to be electronically available.

We first gave seventh and eighth graders in our district e-mail accounts. As soon as they hit high school as freshmen, they expected to have these accounts. And if the ninth graders had e-mail, the rest of the student body wanted it. Fastest technology implementation I'd ever seen.

Services given to the few are soon expected by the many. Not a bad way to get technologies universally adopted.

24

Kids will always know more about some things than you will.

According to a recent listserv posting, a librarian was frustrated because her school's filter denied her class access to Google's search engine. After she voiced her frustration to her class, a student came up and whispered: "You can do the same thing with <http://google.ca> (the unblocked Canadian version of the site). Problem solved.

Many—if not most—kids have more time, more energy, less fear, and greater comfort with technology than we old people ever will. Accept it.

What we bring to the table is not the "how-to" but the "why-to." When my son plunks a digitized movie into a presentation, it's my job to ask "Why?" Does it add to the communication power of the message?

Machines shouldn't do people's jobs.

Here is a personal list of things people rather than technology should do:

- Decide what Internet sites are appropriate and not appropriate.
- Correct someone's grammar.
- Teach kids to read.
- Answer the school telephone.
- Write poetry.

My dad was very mechanical, but never owned an answering machine and complained every time he reached mine. His comment: "If I wanted to talk to a machine, I'd go to the garage and talk to my lawnmower." After going through a dozen menu options when trying to reach some schools, I'm becoming more sympathetic.

Don't ask machines to do tasks that are uniquely human. Artificial intelligence is, after all, artificial.

26

Technology is neither good nor bad. The same hammer can both break windows and build cathedrals.

I call this the rule of technology neutrality. I am constantly amazed at both the technophobes and the technophiles.

- Give kids (or adults) e-mail and they will send tasteless jokes.
- Give them wireless devices and they will pass notes and test-answers.
- Give them photo-editing software and some very silly pictures will result.
- Give them Internet access and they will find sites that are nasty.

This is not new. The first motion pictures made were naughty ones. It probably took the first tool-using ape about 30 seconds to figure out that coconuts and skulls could both be cracked.

I try to remember the Latin expression: *Ex abusu non arguitur in usum.* (The abuse of a thing is no argument against its use.) Anticipate the problems and then adopt the technologies anyway.

27

A policy mantra.

Every now and again I hear: "I can't do that because our technician said I couldn't." Which usually surprises me as Technology Director since I could not remember having made such a decision.

It's at this point I have to ask that teacher or administrator to repeat our policy mantra:

> Technicians do not make policy. Technicians do not make policy. Technicians do not make policy.

Policies and rules regarding technology use should come from educators, not technologists. Of course, smart educators will get lots of input from their techies before making policy.

Keep technicians and paraprofessionals in the loop.

OK, let's be fair here. I just wrote:

> "Policies and rules regarding technology use should come from educators, not technologists."

The corollary to this is that smart educators will make sure technicians and paraprofessionals understand the important role they play in the educational process as well. Such an understanding helps these folks prioritize their often overwhelming work load. It helps them make good technical decisions. It helps give them job satisfaction of a kind their paychecks probably do not.

When a NASA custodian was once asked what his job was, he replied, "To put a man on the moon."

What would your techies say their jobs were?

Philosophy on implementing large technology systems: I'd rather be optimistic than right.

Pardon my French, but implementing, changing or even upgrading any complex technology system is a son of a bitch. I have seen people who are strong, happy and resilient reduced to tears during such a process.

Keep the following in mind:

- The system will eventually work.
- The change serves an important purpose.
- People will not want to go back to the previous system after they have had a chance to get familiar with the new system.
- No amount of training will ever be enough for some people.
- It's not just you—businesses, universities, and technology centers experience problems as well.

I try to remind my boss that a large technology implementation should never be evaluated until it has been in place for at least a year.

Keep the faith. Be optimistic.

30

The first sign of technology literacy is knowing when to use technology and when not to use technology.

I once watched a secretary spend a frustrating thirty minutes trying to get her computer to print an address on an envelope. It was a task that could have been done on a typewriter (or, gasp, even by hand) in less than one minute.

Sadly, I've also seen students go to an Internet terminal and search for a basic fact (the population of Bolivia) for a frustrating thirty minutes only to come up with bad information (from the 1986 CIA Fact Book) when they could have used a recent print almanac and had an accurate answer in minutes.

Technology-literate folks know when to do things the old-fashioned way.

You can't be too thin, too rich, or have too much bandwidth.

Our district's first WAN (Wide Area Network) was created with 14.4 baud modems and nailed-up telephone lines. Pretty cool for 1993. And that network was good enough in those pre-Web days because it was only text that was being pushed and pulled from computer to computer.

I make very few predictions, but one I am confident in making is that we ain't seen nothin' yet when it comes to network use. Already things like video-conferencing, streaming video, off-site application service providers, and IP telephony are making our three-year-old fiber network groan.

Build for the future to the limit of your budget. The future is catching up to you sooner than you might believe.

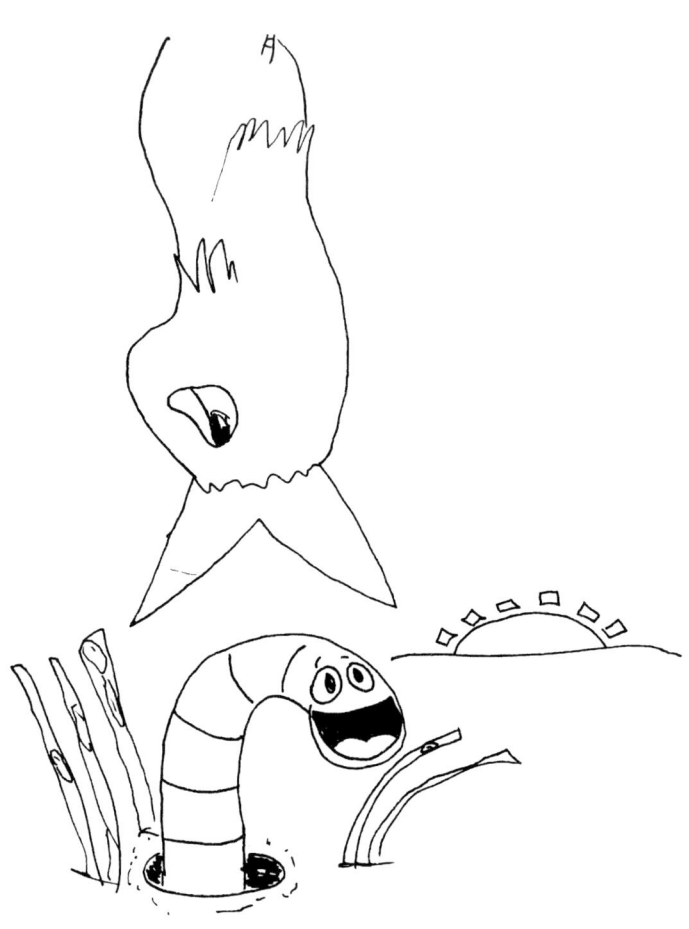

The early worm gets eaten by the bird.

This little homily makes salespersons mad, but has saved me a good deal of agony.

The first question any salesperson pedaling a new product should be asked is, "What are the phone numbers of some school districts successfully using this product—*now?*"

If those numbers aren't forthcoming (and I am in the mood), my next question is, "What is your company willing to pay our district to be a demonstration site?"

It is not my school staff's mission to be a beta tester. It's not our job to make headlines in technology journals.

It's our job to educate our community's children.

You must get the last person on board sooner or later.

Let's call him Bob. When everyone else was reading the building's bulletin sent as an e-mail, Bob was still insisting on a print copy.

You know the reasons.

- Too much effort.
- I don't have time.
- I was never taught how.
- It's not what we've always done.

We continued to print a bulletin for Bob, but made him walk to the office to pick it up each morning. Bob started reading it on e-mail.

The only way to deal with resistors is to make sure the new way of doing things is more convenient than the old way.

Writing and presenting rules

34

Work a little humor into every communication effort.

What did Ole say when the Kinsey Sex Survey called and asked him if he smoked after sex? "Don't know. Never looked."

All right, it's an old joke, but it made you keep on reading. There is really no excuse whatsoever not to inject at least a little humor into every communication effort you make. It's a mistake to confuse dryness with professionalism.

If you want the head paying attention, you have to get the heart involved. Humor is probably the easiest way to evoke an emotional response. (A groan is an emotional response, right?) You can elicit anger, fear or sadness to get attention as well, but for my money smiles do the job better.

Oh. I wouldn't make my jokes any racier than the one above.

35

You can never have
- **too much white space**
- **too big a font, or**
- **too many bullet points.**

My Success Strategy:

- Veni
- Vidi
- Vici
    from J. Caesar's PowerPoint presentation

Written communications that look accessible are more likely to be read. I could condense this entire book into about ten densely packed pages of type. You going to read it? Didn't think so.

My absolutely favorite book on layout and design is Robin Williams's *The Non-Designer's Design Book* (Peachpit Press, 1994).

- Buy it.
- Read it.
- Follow its advice.

36

The greater the simplicity, the greater the understanding.

Each time you add a "step" you confuse an additional 10% of your audience*. If you have a class of ten, when the first person gets to Step 10, I guarantee there will still be someone on Step 1.

There are three easy steps you can take to overcome this:

- Design a graphic that serves as a map.
- Distribute recipe-type handouts for those who fall behind to follow.
- Never have more than three steps.

If you have more than three steps, divide the task into multiple tasks.

Look hard at what you are trying to teach and extract the important stuff, leaving behind the merely "nice to know" stuff and the "I know more than you do, ain't I hot?" stuff. Teach the important stuff and let folks figure out the rest on their own.

* Remember that 86% of statistics are made up.

37

Graphics rule!

Johnson's Hierarchy of Technology Needs

Empowered Students

Enhanced Teaching

Extensive Resources

Effective Administartion

Established Infrastructure

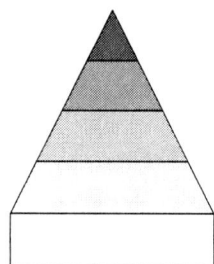

There are more visual learners than meet the eye. (Sorry, couldn't resist.)

A good, even simple, graphic can go a surprisingly long way toward increasing a learner's understanding of a concept.

Dr. Gary Hartzell, author of *Building Influence for the School Librarian,* uses a simple graphic of a state-fair ribbon like one you'd find on a prize-winning hog to highlight presentation slides that convey key points. I see the ribbon; I write the point down. It works.

You can put all the pretty clothes you want to on your dog, but he's still a dog.

PowerPoint, HyperStudio and other multimedia presentation tools are dangerous devices. Users, especially students, have a tendency to spend way too much time on a presentation's appearance at the expense of its content. Popular speaker and author Jamie McKenzie calls this "power-pointlessness."

Good assessment tools for presentations describe three components:

- How good is the content?
- How effective is the speaker?
- Did the technology help clarify the message?

Lots more points should be given to the first two areas than the last.

There are many good sources available that deal with giving effective multimedia presentations. I'm just picking a few things that really grind my gears. And these are things both high-priced speakers and third graders often do. Thanks for letting me vent.

First Law of Presentations: Show your audience pictures of happy, productive children and they will believe almost anything you tell them.

I hate clip art, especially clip art I've seen about a million times.

Illustrate your slides with pictures of actual happy, smilin', gettin'-educated children taken with a digital camera. If you're worried about parental permission, run the picture through a photo-editing filter until the individual is unrecognizable. You'll even look talented.

Or find a student with a knack for cartooning and buy the work.

40

Second Law of Presentations: Audiences would rather see your face than your backside.

It is amazing how all the sins made by those using overhead transparencies have made the transition to electronic slides quite nicely.

Small illegible text and poorly reproduced cartoons are still popular in PowerPoint presentations.

But it is the overhead of solid text read in a drone by presenter who turns to face the screen that has really ported over well.

Unless you are Jennifer Lopez, your backside will probably not contribute to your message in a powerful way.

Third Law of Presentations: A misspelling in 48 point type is more noticeable than a misspelling in 12 point type.

The slide read:

Welcome back to Overshoe Pubic Schools

Somebody trusted a spelling checker.

I am a terrible proofreader of my own work. Thank heavens for editors, secretaries and spouses. If you do make a grammatical error, adopt the Navajo blanket-weavers' philosophy that things perfect are an insult to the gods.

42

Fourth Law of Presentations: Be consistent.

This one is tough. Audiences will not understand on a conscious level why a presentation is bothersome to them, but it will be if the elements it contains are inconsistent.

Keep it simple. Throughout the presentation:

- Use the same fonts and colors for headings and text.
- Never use more than one sans serif font (headings) and one serif font (body).
- Use the same size font for each heading and vary the text size as little as possible.
- Start the heading and the text in exactly the same place on every slide. (Use guides to help do this.)
- Left or right justify everything. Centered text is weak and hard to read.

Try this with one of your slide shows. You will be amazed at how much more professional you'll look.

43

Fifth Law of Presentations: Beware of some compliments.

I used to be pleased, but now I am worried when the questions from workshop attendees go like this:

- How did you make them there bullet points fly in?
- How'd ya get the program to make that funny noise?
- What fonts did you use?
- Do you like Macs or Wind'ers?

These comments tell me the group did not get the message I intended about technology use. They were paying more attention to the slide show than to me. I'd created my own little digital Frankenstein. Don't do it.

My most worrisome compliment, quite sincerely given, was: "Doug, just watching you set up was the best part of your presentation."

It's hard not to get a big head.

Administration of anything rules

44

Rules only work with the rational.

- Reasonable rules work with reasonable people.
- Petty rules breed resentment.
- Even the best rules only work with rational people.

I've never worked with or in a group of any size that had a 100% rationality rate. (Of course, my personal rationality rate isn't 100% either.)

I don't know what you do about that. But knowing it, I hope, makes you feel better.

45

Three rules of policy writing.

- Never write a policy unless it is absolutely unavoidable.
- Never write a policy from scratch that you can borrow from someone else.
- Never write a policy that does not describe how it benefits the students in your school.

46

The Law of Effective Supervision.

Only hire people who don't need to be supervised.

I am the world's worst supervisor. If I can't:

- give a person a task, a timeline, and adequate resources;
- turn them loose;
- and expect good results,

I really don't want them working for me.

I've been good at hiring such folks. One question I always ask during job interviews is: "Can you describe a major project you've undertaken of which you are proud?"

It doesn't much matter if the project described is building a new outhouse or teaching one's parakeet to sing the "Star Spangled Banner." But if the interviewee can't come up with something, that person doesn't get hired.

Maybe this attitude comes from not liking to be supervised.

47

The Doughnut System™.

Just because one does not supervise employees, doesn't mean that one should not be evaluating them. Our printer Greg helped me formulate the Doughnut Employee Evaluation System™.

Here is how it works:

- Let if be known that the best way teachers and administrators can express their appreciation for work above and beyond the call of duty by an employee of your department is to bring that employee a box of pastries.
- The above pastries are shared with others in the department, custodians, and visitors.
- The boss keeps track of how many such boxes are given in any employee's name. The more doughnuts, the better the evaluation.

As supervisor, take credit for one doughnut from each box since you had the intelligence to hire such outstanding individuals.

Whine prevention.

An old principals' riddle:

> What is the difference between a puppy and a teacher?
> The puppy stops whining when you let it in your door.

(Don't tell the joke above in the teachers' lounge.)

The best advice ever given about whining is in Richard Moran's book *Never Confuse a Memo with Reality* (HarperBusiness, 1993). He writes: "Never take a problem to your boss without some solutions. You are getting paid to think, not to whine."

The administrator's job is to create problem-solvers, not problem articulators.

"And what do you think should be done about that?" is a good phrase to practice using.

If you can't solve a person's problem, at least let them know you're aware of the problem.

There are problems that do have solutions, but that can't be solved immediately. My techs are often stymied by strange technology behaviors. But a quick e-mail that says, "I am aware of the problem and am working on. I'll get back to you tomorrow," helps.

Internationally-known speaker and author Ian Jukes responds to all e-mails he receives within forty-eight hours. He's a pretty big fish and probably doesn't have to do that. But it is very cool that he does.

The majority of the problems in our "technology" department stem not from the technology itself, but from poor communications.

But we're working on it and will get back to you when we've come up with a solution.

Teaching rules

A project not worth doing is not worth doing well.

Kids have the capacity for sophisticated thinking about ethical issues. One emerging line of reasoning that all teachers should consider is:

"Cheating is OK when the assignment has no purpose beyond busy work."

If a student has the choice between spending time:

• Practicing lay-ups
• Putting in a few extra hours at work
• Reading about personal interests
• Doing your stupid assignment

who can blame him if he finds ways to minimize the work involved in what he views as lacking value?

Same attitude I take toward state reports.

Rule of Restructuring Education with Technology: the real changes are in teaching practices, not technology.

- Using a word processor to create prettier worksheets is not integrating technology into the classroom.
- Teaching kids how to design a multimedia presentation devoid of content is not productive.
- Providing Internet access to students without instructing them in its use and proper purpose is a waste of resources.
- Putting kids in front of a reading or math workbook that has been moved at great expense to a computer screen is dehumanizing.

Only slowly has the profession come to realize that technology "integration" really means moving to project-centered, authentic, collaborative, and creative focus in the classroom.

Technology can help catalyze the replacement of the 3 Rs of Rote, Restraint and Regurgitation with the 5 Cs of Child-centered, Creativity, Computers, Collaboration, and Communication. (And maybe 6 if you add Compassion.)

52

Law of Assessment: You'll only get what you want if you can describe what you want.

Speaker and consultant Debbie Silver has a perfect term for the kids who have the ability to read their teacher's minds. She calls them little "bow-heads."

You know them. The little girls and boys who seem to instinctively know just what the teacher wants on any given assignment. The ones who always get their papers displayed on the bulletin board. The ones who get into the college of their choice.

Debbie and others are out to help level the playing field for those of us who lacked such intuition by advocating the use of good assessment tools that serve as a guide to the completion and quality of schoolwork. These checklists and rubrics are given at the beginning of an assignment and used to check progress during it.

Speaking from experience, parents of less than academically over-achieving children appreciate such tools as well.

Don't be surprised if you don't get quality work if you can't describe it.

If you want creativity you have to ask for it.

My son once came home with the assignment:

"Write a paper about bats."

I nearly suggested he copy the entry from an encyclopedia and tell his teacher that someone else had already done this job. Instead we worked on how we could (and whether we should) attract bats to our own backyard.

I have very little sympathy for teachers who complain about plagiarism but who continue to give assignments that don't ask for any kind of originality.

Oh, for the record, it's always been the teacher who drew the short straw who got my son as a student—through no fault of his own.

54

If it works with third graders, it'll fly with adults.

I did not make it through Algebra II in high school and I remain math-phobic. But I aced my graduate statistics class. All thanks to the instructor.

My guess is that Bill understood that folks who take a statistics class on Saturday mornings in the spring are there to meet a program requirement, not to become statisticians. As a former junior high math teacher, Bill used the same techniques with us that he did with 12-year-olds:

- Lots of review
- Lots of relevant examples
- Lots of applied practice
- Lots of humor
- Lots more review
- Clear expectations of what would be on the test.

I can't tell a T-score from a standard deviation from the norm today, but I can tell you that good teaching is good teaching whether it is with adults or kids.

Children will be in genuine danger if certain skills are not taught.

Instructions on using dangerous technologies are accompanied by training on how to use them safely. Such technologies include:

- Scuba diving
- Shooting a gun
- Driving a car

I am guessing that skydiving could be added to the list, but I am not about to find out.

At what point does the use of information technologies fall into the dangerous category? Do kids:

- Find pro-anorexia sites on the web?
- Meet pedophiles in chat rooms?
- Locate inaccurate information about STDs?

The ability to evaluate information and navigate the Internet safely must be taught to all students. To do less is no more responsible than handing them a loaded gun.

56

Integrate technology into your worst units.

Every teacher I know has units that are weak. When I taught seventh grade English, I dreaded the poetry unit. Kids didn't like it and I didn't like it. It stunk.

A big mistake many teachers make is plunking some technology-related project smack into their best units, the strong ones that have great activities, are supported by wonderful resources, and are loved by the students.

This may come as a surprise, but technology-enhanced projects do not always go well the first time. And by placing them in a strong part of your curriculum, you run a high risk of screwing up a good thing.

Plunk these projects into the worst area of your curriculum. Things can only get better.

57

The franchise dilemma.

Why do classroom projects work well for the originator and not when others try them? It's because of what I call the "franchise dilemma." In the restaurant business, there are many great local restaurants, but when an attempt is made to franchise them, only a very small percentage are successful. Why? Because it's almost impossible to export the passion and artistry of the person who made the first restaurant so splendid.

Teachers have stunningly successful projects because of their passion for the topic or the method they used. One fellow each year has his kids research the history of a local building and turn the research into articles for the local paper. When others have tried this they don't seem to make it "go."

The best we can do is offer examples of projects which have worked for others and then glean the kernel of pedagogy that made them so successful—relevance, leveraging the popularity of technology, group work, effective skill attainment, etc.

We can't "teacher-proof" teaching. Without genuine personal investment in what and how we teach, the job just becomes a mindless set of actions.

58

Teach what you use.

In 1982, the board of the district in which I was librarian and English teacher decided to buy an Apple II computer instead of library books. I was not happy. And instead of processing books with my three days of extended contract time, I taught myself the AppleWriter word processing program. At the end of those three days, I thought "Wow!"

I was suddenly no longer captive of some of my own writing limitations: bad handwriting, crummy spelling, and poor keyboarding skills that made revision painful and time-consuming. My stuff looked professional. I was liberated.

Ten seconds later I realized that everyday I taught about seventy-five kids who might also experience such liberation. Technology use in schools suddenly made sense.

Teach with the technology that personally empowers *you*.

Library rules

59

The number of students in the library media center will always be in inverse proportion to the importance of anyone who stops by to visit.

It never fails. There are a thousand kids in the library third hour. When the superintendent and board members drop by on a facilities inspection an hour later, the place is a ghost town.

There is not one damn thing you can do to keep this from happening.

There are things you can do to counteract such mistaken perceptions, however:

- Keep the library as full of kids as possible as many hours as possible.
- Make communications and marketing a top priority.
- Issue invitations to important people to visit during exciting times.

There are enough things in life that cannot be anticipated or controlled. Work on the things you can.

60

Life-long impressions of libraries are formed very young.

I once had a superintendent brag to me that he obtained his college degrees without ever setting foot in a library. (And this was in pre-Internet days.)

"I thought there was something special about you," I tactfully replied.

There are people who don't like libraries. My suspicion is that they were frightened by a librarian as children.

The kids we bark at, ignore, or chase from our libraries today are our teachers, school board members, legislators and referendum voters of tomorrow.

What goes around, comes around.

61

The library rule rule.

Never have more than three rules for your media center. These are mine:

- Be doing something productive
- Be doing it in a way that allows others to be productive
- Be respectful of other people and their property.

That's it.

The beauty of this is that nearly every behavior, both of commission and omission, can be judged according to these rules.

If your library has a list of a dozen or more rules (Don't eat the library books. Don't poke others with sharp objects. Don't sharpen your pencil more than 3 times within 45 minutes. Don't moon the librarian.), rethink your strategy.

Teaching kids to examine their own behavior and apply simple codes of conduct to a variety of circumstances is not a bad thing to do.

The librarian is the library.

The best facility, the best resources, the best budget and the greatest curriculum do not make a great library program.

The single key ingredient of a successful program is a library media specialist who is approachable, collaborative, and supportive of staff and students.

If the right media person is in place, the rest of the "stuff" follows.

63

The paraprofessional is often the face of the library.

When Mrs. Palardy was my library clerk, I was called Mr. Palardy about half the time. Of course, Mrs. Palardy was also frequently called Mrs. Johnson.

Library patrons, especially kids, don't know and don't care who the "professional" librarian in the media center is. We are all "librarians" in their eyes.

So?

When is the last time you provided a staff development opportunity for your paraprofessional? If the clerk is crabby, what do the kids think about your library? Have you given your paraprofessional a chance to be creative or try a new task lately?

Behind every successful librarian is a competent paraprofessional. Never underestimate the para's importance.

There is no reason not to have a budget.

Too many library media specialists confuse having a budget with having a fully funded budget.

It is our job to create yearly budget proposals that realistically reflect the resources we feel are necessary to run a program that contributes to student achievement. It may be unlikely that the budget is fully funded, but that doesn't mean it shouldn't be submitted.

How is a principal going to know what you need and why you need it unless you tell him?

Schools, administrators and states have lots of money—more than enough to support quality library media programs. They may not choose to fund such programs, but they have the money to do so.

Help them make good choices.

65

Be virtual.

Don't fight the fact that kids would rather access information online than in a physical library. Quite frankly, so would I. Even the most convenient library is never as close as my computer.

Every library needs a web page that guides its patrons to reliable and relevant resources. Librarians should be taking and answering requests and questions by e-mail.

Learning to make web pages is not rocket science.

Tom Peters observes, "If you don't like change, you'll like irrelevance even less."

Accentuate the things you can do that the Internet can't.

The Internet has also threatened other services. Nobody is picking on libraries. What do these entities still offer that their online counterparts cannot?

- Bookstores -> Inviting atmosphere
- Schools -> Child containment
- Travel agents -> Expertise/time savings
- Banks -> Traditional services enhanced with online services

Physical spaces are still relevant, even in an increasingly virtual world. But they have to be inviting, personal and worth the trip.

67

Be a teacher first, librarian second.

Schools need only two things: students and teachers. Everything else is optional.

We need to be teachers. That means:

- Having a curriculum that only we teach that is considered valuable by the community we serve.
- Having a concrete set of benchmarks that can be objectively assessed.
- Directly teaching students.
- Assessing student performance.
- Reporting student performance back to students and their parents.
- Having a required teaching license.

These are all things teachers do. And we should too.

68

Don't advocate for libraries.

It's self-serving.

   Advocate for library users.

Poor librarians reflect on all of us.

Alice couldn't cut it in the classroom.

Alice couldn't be fired.

Alice was made the school librarian.

Because such a path into the profession has not been un-common in the past, principals and teachers may have come in contact with untrained, incompetent librarians. Unfortunately, they still exist.

We need actively to encourage those folks to find another line of work. We need to tighten up entrance requirements to library schools. We need to police our own ranks.

If only we could get these people into Congress—both professions would be vastly improved.

70

Weed.

I once took over a job for a woman who had been a school librarian for twenty years. During her tenure, she never threw a thing away. Most of the books were so old they could legally drink and many could have gotten Social Security.

I know this because the bottom-left drawer of her desk contained about a dozen years of the *Sports Illustrated* swimsuit editions. Happy, happy Doug.

I envisioned Evelyn's dilemma: "I can't put this out where children will see it, but I can't throw it away." It must have cost her sleepless nights.

Poorly weeded collections are not the sign of poor budgets but of poor librarianship. Small but high-quality collections are the sign of inadequate budgets.

Parting thoughts

Everyone suffers from IDS.

My relationship to technology is exemplified by the bewilderment I feel every time I use my garage door opener.

It has three buttons of which only one has any purpose that I can determine. I believe the opener was designed to purposely aggravate my symptoms of IDS—Intelligence Deficit Syndrome. I am just not smart enough to use technology well.

Who knows what wonders and pleasures could come from learning to use the functions of those other two buttons? Is self-actualization just one combination of button pushes away? Someday I may just need to find and read the manual.

But for now I will use the one big button this weak mind does understand, open and close the garage door, and remain firmly, if mistakenly, committed to the idea that I can be a fully-functional, happy person despite how intelligence-deficit technology makes me feel.

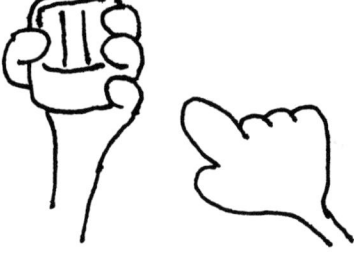

72

Take your job seriously, but not yourself.

Gil Carlson, from St. Peter, Minnesota, gave me the advice above when I was working for him. I liked the fact that he followed it himself.

I like to ask myself at the end of the day if I did anything that might make a good story one day: one I can tell at the supper table, to my grandkids, to the guys around the campfire, or to the nurse who changes my drool bucket at the nursing home.

Story-less people are folks who take themselves way too seriously, fearful of looking foolish, appearing ignorant, or being wrong. The challenges we've faced, the problems we've solved, the good we've tried to do, and especially the bumps and detours we've encountered along the way are the basis of interesting tales.

Do something today that will make your story more interesting.

73

There is a role for old people in technology.

John Lubbock, a nineteenth-century astronomer, once wrote:

> There are three great questions which in life we have
> to ask over and over again to answer:
> • Is it right or wrong?
> • Is it true or false?
> • Is it beautiful or ugly?

Our education ought to help us to answer these questions.

I think of those words often when I hear educators worry about kids being more adept and comfortable with technology than those of us who were growing up when the earth was still cooling.

No matter how sophisticated the N-Geners are technologically, in matters of ethics, aesthetics, and other important realms of value and judgment, they are, after all, still green. By virtue of our training and life experiences, we can apply the standards of older technologies (the pencil, the podium, the book) to those that are now technology enhanced. And we'd better. Given the choice of having Socrates or Bill Gates as a teacher, I know whom I would choose.

Upstream cost, downstream savings.

Now and again it strikes me that a picture in my house is hanging crooked, and each time I notice this I take a few seconds to straighten that picture out.

Conceptually I know that if I took five minutes, got a hammer, a nail, a pencil, and a level, I could attach a second nail and never have to straighten the damn picture again.

But like most people, I never seem to have the upstream time it takes to realize downstream time savings. Human nature, I suppose.

That is probably the major reason technology is so difficult to get busy educators to use. Convincing someone that learning to create a pdf file of an often-requested document, load it to a website, and create a link to it—thereby saving all the time it takes to locate, print, and send the document manually over and over again—is a tough sell.

About as tough as it is to convince me to go get the hammer.

75

Advice to children and singles.

Tom Weller has a delightful little book called *Minims*, now out of print but available (as of Spring 2003) at <users.rcn.com/kbruhns/minims/>. This is how he defines a *minim*:

> minim ['mInIm] *n*: a statement expressed in proverbial or sentential form but having no general application or practical use whatever—compare MAXIM.

I have come up with only one minim: Marry for money; repent in leisure.

If you follow that single piece of advice, you can completely stop worrying about lots of other rules, including the ones in this book.

A short list of mind-bending books every educator should read.

The really scary books are not about ghosts and vampires. They challenge beliefs we may long have held near and dear. Read these and be afraid—very afraid.

1. *Teaching as a Subversive Activity.* Neil Postman. As good as when it was written over forty years ago and even more critically needed today. Remind yourself why you went into teaching.

2. *Language in Thought and Action.* S. I. Hayakawa. How language controls us.

3. *School's Out.* Lewis J. Perelman. The educational, structural, and political changes Perelman predicted are coming true. Just more slowly.

4. *Punished by Rewards.* Alfie Kohn. The most compassionate education writer alive explains why extrinsic motivation harms students.

5. *Savage Inequality.* Jonathan Kozol. Explains the difference between schools for the governors and the governed. In which do you work?

6. *Failure to Connect.* Jane M. Healy.
   Computers being used badly in schools. Tell me it
   isn't so!

7. *Future of Success.* Robert B. Reich.
   Readable exploration of work as our students will
   know it.

8. *The Mac (PC) is Not a Typewriter.* Robin Williams.
   One read through this and your printed work will
   look good.

9. *Things That Make Us Smart: Defending
   Human Attributes in the Age of the Machine.*
   Donald A. Norman.
   Bad engineering and design is behind the frustration
   with technology that many normal people feel.

   10. *Results.* Mike Schmoker.
       An intelligent, practical approach to the power of
       educational measurement and accountability.

Doug's other books—available from Linworth Publishing www.linworth.com.

The Indispensable Librarian

The Indispensable Teacher's Guide to Computer Skills (2nd edition)

Teaching Right from Wrong in the Digital Age: An Ethics Guide for Parents, Teachers, Librarians, and Others Who Care about Computer-Using Young People

Workshops and Presentations

Actual comments from workshop attendees and not from my mother:

- You have been a breath of fresh air. It's obvious that you know this stuff as well as (or better than) most of the experts, but you manage to keep it entertaining. Thank you so much—I was beginning to wonder if somebody like me, who sometimes sees the world in a slightly skewed fashion, would be able to fit in. You have set a wonderful example—professional and yet funny. A perfect mix!
- It's a joy to be part of a workshop when the presenter clearly enjoys what he does and encourages and values direct input from his audience.
- Doug Johnson is worth the entire conference.
- With an eye toward student achievement, I anticipate building a stronger and even more effective program. Wonderful plan and ideas.
- This workshop started so many ideas churning (some old and some new). I will use ideas to promote the media center and help our kids continue to grow.
- Doug Johnson is knowledgeable and has a humorous personality. Handouts will be useful throughout the school year. Of tremendous benefit to smaller districts.

- Doug Johnson was well-organized and sincere. He definitely transmitted his passion of a successful library program to our group.
- It is wonderful to have a workshop addressing unique needs of library programs. Programs like these help us focus on impacting student learning.
- Just wanted to add my vote of thanks and appreciation to those of your other enthusiastic fans. Your ideas have stayed with me.
- This workshop was EXCELLENT! Very entertaining, but also very, very relevant to school.
- Energizing—great ideas, wonderful handouts. Most importantly—places from which I can move and do my own thing.
- Many examples given today can be used at work as well as in one's personal life.
- It got me motivated to use more technology in the classroom.
- It was nice to be able to laugh and learn at the same time.

A complete list of presentations I give can be found at: www.doug-johnson.com

Doug Johnson grew up on a farm in Iowa where he spent an ungodly amount of his formative years developing his manure-shoveling skills.

These skills have continued to be useful. He has been the Director of Media and Technology for the Mankato (MN) Public Schools since 1991 and has served as an adjunct faculty member of Minnesota State University, Mankato since 1990. His continued employment still amazes his high school teachers.

Doug's classroom teaching and school library experiences have included work in grades K-12 in schools both here and in Saudi Arabia.

He is the author of three other books and his regular column appears in *Library Media Connection* magazine. His articles have appeared in over thirty books and periodicals. (All of Doug's writings have recently been approved by the FDA as a non-addictive sleep aid.)

Doug has conducted workshops and given presentations for over 100 organizations throughout the United States as well as in Malaysia, Kenya, Thailand, Germany, Qatar, Canada and the wilds of Minnesota. And has lived to tell about it.

Visit Doug's website at www.doug-johnson.com for more information and pictures of his grandson.

Brady Johnson, illustrator, is a senior in high school and cleans his own bathroom. When not playing video games, he sometimes helps his father learn about the way the world really works.

And he is a terrific guy!